If I Were an
Astronaut

by Eric Braun   illustrated by Sharon Harmer

Special thanks to our advisers for their expertise:

Joe Tanner
Former Astronaut
Aerospace Engineering Sciences
University of Colorado at Boulder

Terry Flaherty, Ph.D.
Professor of English
Minnesota State University, Mankato

Picture Window Books
Minneapolis, Minnesota

Editor: Shelly Lyons
Designer: Tracy Davies
Page Production: Melissa Kes
Art Director: Nathan Gassman
Editorial Director: Nick Healy
Creative Director: Joe Ewest
The illustrations in this book were created with digital and traditional drawing and painting.

Picture Window Books
1710 Roe Crest Drive
North Mankato, MN 56003
877-845-8392
www.capstonepub.com

Library of Congress Cataloging-in-Publication Data
Braun, Eric, 1971-
If I were an astronaut / by Eric Braun ; illustrated by Sharon Harmer.
p. cm. — (Dream big!)
Includes bibliographical references and index.
ISBN 978-1-4048-5534-2 (library binding)
ISBN 978-1-4048-5710-0 (paperback)
1. Astronauts—Juvenile literature. 2. Astronautics—Juvenile literature. I. Harmer, Sharon, ill. II. Title. TL793.B72 2010
  629.45—dc22   2009006883

If I were an astronaut, I would fly a spacecraft in outer space.

If I were an astronaut, I would feel the G's. Gravity would pin me to my seat as I blasted off. My arms and legs would feel like concrete as I rose into space.

If I were an astronaut, I would dock my ship to the Space Station. I would gently settle the shuttle into place.

Be careful! Lighten up on the thrusters!

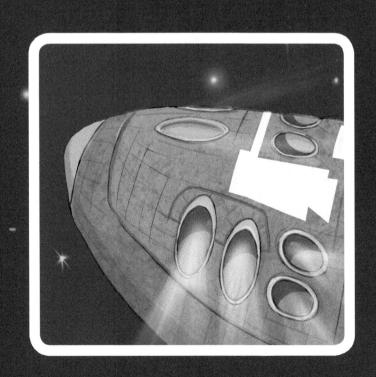

If I were an astronaut, I would be part of a super team. I would work with astronauts and scientists from all around the world. We would learn from each other and help each other. We would have the greatest jobs we could imagine.

If I were an astronaut, I would run a
robotic arm. I would lift a huge truss
from the shuttle. The part would be
added to the Space Station.

Don't bump it! Don't drop it!

10

The International Space Station is a satellite. It is a place where astronauts take turns living for months at a time. The Space Station continues to grow. Spacecraft launch from Earth with new parts. Parts are handled with a robotic arm.

If I were an astronaut, I would take a space walk. I would fix a section of the Space Station. Stars, planets, and deep space would be all around.

What a view!

If I were an astronaut, I would try to keep my food from floating away! Some food, such as spaghetti or scrambled eggs, would be dried. I would add water before I warmed it in the oven.

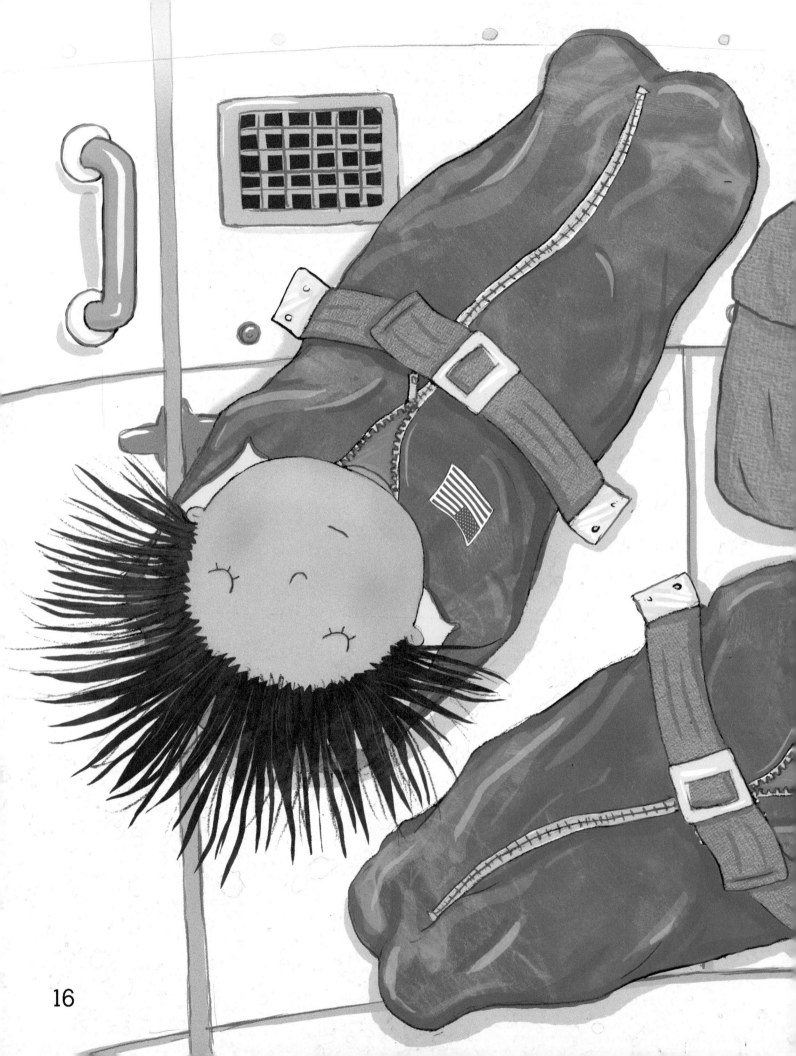

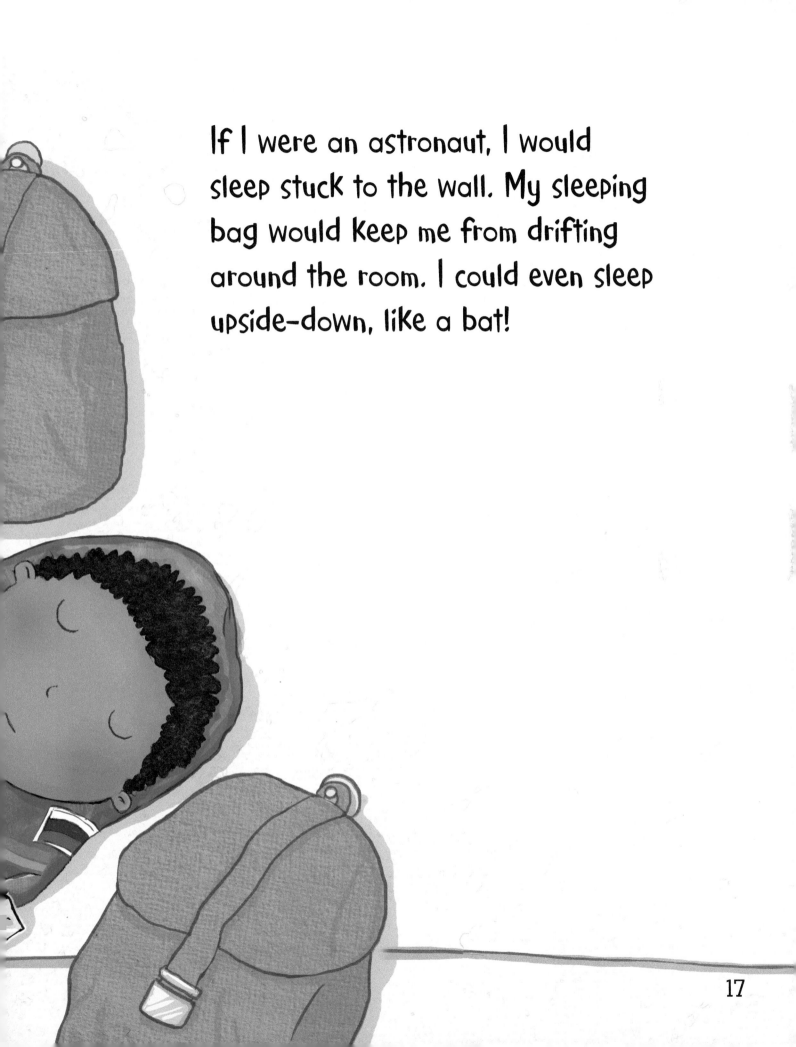

If I were an astronaut, I would sleep stuck to the wall. My sleeping bag would keep me from drifting around the room. I could even sleep upside-down, like a bat!

If I were an astronaut, I would do cool science experiments. I might even discover important new medicines.

Experiments on crystals in space have taught scientists how to make better medicines and even computer chips.

If I were an astronaut, each day would be an adventure. I would visit outer space and see amazing things. I would live in the Space Station for months at a time.

I would have a blast!

How do you get to be an Astronaut?

People who want to be astronauts study lots of math and science. They get hundreds of hours of experience flying. They exercise a lot, so they are in great shape. People who want to be astronauts have to be patient and believe in themselves. It takes a long time and a lot of work to be an astronaut.

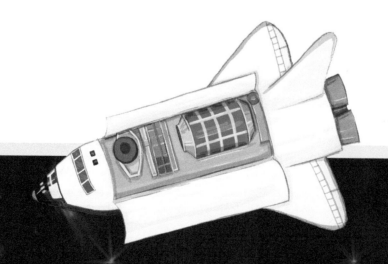

Glossary

dock—to join with

experiments—scientific tests that are used to prove or discover something

G's—short for G-force; this is how acceleration is measured

gravity—the force that pulls objects toward Earth's surface

launch—to send something into outer space

robotic arm—a mechanical arm operated by an astronaut

satellite—a spacecraft that circles around Earth or another body in outer space

shuttle—a spacecraft that takes people and supplies into outer space and back

spacecraft—a vehicle that travels in outer space

Space Station—short for the International Space Station (ISS); the Space Station is a research laboratory that orbits Earth; it is a joint project shared by the space agencies from the United States, Russia, Canada, Japan, and European nations

thrusters—rocket engines that control how a spacecraft moves

truss—a piece of framework that supports the larger structure

To Learn More

More Books to Read

Aldrin, Buzz. *Reaching for the Moon*. New York: Harper Collins, 2005.

Bredeson, Carmen. *What Do Astronauts Do?* Berkeley Heights, N.J.: Enslow Elementary, 2008.

McCarthy, Meghan. *Astronaut Handbook*. New York: Alfred A. Knopf, 2008.

Internet Sites

FactHound offers a safe, fun way to find Internet sites related to this book. All of the sites on FactHound have been researched by our staff.

Here's all you do:

Visit *www.facthound.com*

FactHound will fetch the best sites for you!

Index

Look for all of the books in the Dream Big! series:

If I Were a Ballerina

If I Were a Major League Baseball Player

If I Were an Astronaut

If I Were the President